For Jem

CONTENTS

LOVE - AND ALL THAT

FAMILY AND FRIENDS

MISCELLANY

THE THIRD AGE

A FEW WORDS WITH MYSELF

INTRODUCTION

Cecilia Chance is a poet with a very individual tone of voice - and with it she takes her reader down many paths. Her outlook on the world is immediately engaging and wonderfully unsentimental. These are poems with a nicely unobtrusive message - some are moving, others touching, many will make you laugh out loud. With her years of experience in so many walks of life it is refreshing not only to uncover - as might be expected - several pearls of wisdom, but also to marvel at the youthful freshness maintained throughout a collection spanning some thirty-five years.

As a composer I found that as I started to read *When I am Old I shall grow Roses* a musical response had started to form and by the end (with its wonderful twist) I was determined to set it to music! But all the poems command reading and I am confident that you will find food for thought, memorable images and lines to store in the memory within these pages. It will soon become clear that her family are the lynch-pin of Cecilia's life and so it is very appropriate that the volume is delightfully illustrated by her sixteen-year-old grandson Michael.

Geraint Lewis
Dygwyl Dewi - St. David's Day 2003

Love - and all That

I WENT TO MYCENAE....

I went to Mycenae with a neat, packaged, set of emotions,
Ducked through the Lion Gate full of guidebook notions,
But the fact was, it was raining, everything dripped, and my red
Unsuitable coat clung, and rivulets ran from your head.

Had we strayed onto the wrong set? Had we mistaken
Old Agamemnon's fortress for some God-forsaken
Cloud-lapped Valhalla? There was not a sound - not a sound -
To wound the ancient stones heaped on that haunted ground.

Only the squeak of our sandals, as we tried to trace
Through wet grass the old well, and find the burial place
And the bridal chamber. Wiser tourists had taken cover
- Even that nice professorial American, that lover
Of old stones with his pockets full of pebbles - well,
He'd settled for a haircut, back at the hotel.

But I must see Mycenae, and you, who had been before,
Wanted to watch me looking; to share what I saw.
Only I could not find a proper seriousness,
For the place was full of flowers, awash in the grass;
Pools of red anemone there for the taking
And succulent green things growing, and almond
        blossom breaking.

It was not a day for ruins. Neither could compose
Faces or flower-drenched arms into a classic pose.
Only now, long after, great waves and torrents flood
My mind when I remember - yes, that is where I stood!
I was there! Yes, we passed through that haunted place,
And I only saw the flowers and you only saw my face.

HE SAID HE LOVED HER FOR HER SOUL

He said he loved her for her soul.
'What is my soul?' she said.
'It is that glowing flame that lives
When sinful flesh is fled.'
She left him for a better man
Who kept her warm in bed.

PELICAN

Comfort, gentle pelican
- When all your store is gone,
For your young, peck out your breast,
Brute love is tenderest,
O tenderer, tenderer far
Than measured words are.

LUNCH AT LUIGI'S

'Well?' you said, 'Well - how are you?' We sat down,
Studied the menu, ordered *steak au poivre*,
The wine list took your customary frown,
I watched your face and fiddled with a glove.
'Sorry I'm late,' you said. 'I barely made it
- A tiresome meeting.' Step by step you told me
How it had been. I was attentive - laid it
Loyally on, feeling your need to hold me.

At first I could not reach you, I was caught,
Ravelled in words, meshed in meaningless chatter.
I could find no way to untie the knot
And every moment it was getting later.
Only with the coffee your eyes undid the thread.
I flew, heart to your heart, and jumped into your head.

ISLANDS

Go on. Smile at me. Turn your head. I feel
Abandoned by your eyes. Must there still be
Locked places? Wounds I have no power to heal
Or love to allay? Oh why can't you make me
Into a mop, to sop grief, or a rough
Rug to smother it? The words I say
Are waste, and what I am is not enough,
Never enough, for still you turn away.

So we make islands. Not pleasant places,
No myrtle groves, warm thickets of sweet briars,
Refreshing streams - no hive for the honey-bee.
No, we make deserts and with closed-up faces
Watch the smoke rising from old signal fires
That we lit once, hoping someone would see.

SOMETHING TERRIBLE HAS HAPPENED

It was the April sun that gives no heat
That drew us to the beach. It was the sun,
And so we went; to walk and be together.

It was your last day, and so most precious.
Linking arms, we headed into the wind
And salt glare. Sand blistered our faces.

It was not a day for the daffodils
Or for small land birds. Only the screaming gulls
On their salt pillows were comfortable.

It was a time for repeating over and over
Old vows that lovers use. But the wind
Stole our words. We faltered and fell silent.

It was then, looking seaward for distraction
I saw the sanderlings planing the shoreline,
Birds without shadows, incorporeal, like moths.

- It was their weightless flight and their deft way
With the waves. I ached for the day's end,
Yearning to join them. For you to be gone.

It was your last day, and so most precious,
But all week she had plagued me, my sly fox,
Tracking our footsteps through the marram grass.

It was nobody's fault that my red vixen
Chose that moment to bite off your head. But
Once done, it can never be put back again.

SO THAT'S IT THEN

There. Out you go,
Biting the dust!
Love, was it?
Or dabbling lust?
Those tiger paws,
Now weak as kittens,
Unlearn the jungle's
Authoritative patterns
And wearily
Creep home.

Family and Friends

BOY, SLEEPING

I love your night-time hair.
Mouse-brown, you smell like a brown
Mouse, or kitten fur by a fire,
Or hayseed the wind sends down.

You never seem to sleep yourself cool.
Little girls, remote,
Cool as lily petals,
Sleep as if they know that sleep is good.
For you, rest is fuel,
Not the heart's food.
Furiously sucking your thumb
You draw sleep down through your blood.

Sometimes I come,
Stoop over you,
Ache to see how your arm curls
To its pillow haven.
Fear unfurls,
Darkness hides the sea,
The unsparing sea
You must sail upon.

A dark sail flutters,
But you sleep on.

MUMMY - IF A LION COMES

Mummy - if a lion comes,
A real lion, when I'm at school,
Shut both the doors.
Don't look out at his fierce face
Or his sharp claws.

Then, when I come home,
With my satchel and my reading book,
I'll get a knife
And I'll kill him, Mum,
But you mustn't look
While I take his life.

FAMILY PORTRAITS

i. KATHARINE

- Such a pity the *boy* has the eyes,
Said some dumbo friend of my grandmother's
In my aunt's hearing.
(She was thirteen at the time.)

The words rooted deep.

Fifty years later
They still bore
Their hard fruit.

ii. EUSTACE

He would have become like his mother.
Her long face, straight nose. A horse person.
Handsome, high-bred,
The natural leader
Beloved of housemasters.

He was gifted beyond the common run,
The unmarked face uncommonly beautiful.

Shaded by the peaked officer's cap
With it's Grenadier star (a crack regiment)
His half smile is as gentle
As a priest at a sacrament.

On the field of battle, his
Rank placed him up front,
Where he fell,
Doing his duty, leading seasoned men
Who mourned him, the citation said,
Like a son.

He was nineteen years old
And Armistice Day a bare month off.

THE OLD PHOTOGRAPH

Sister Patricia C.S.M.V. 1891-1987

You control your own space,
Your rapt composure
Must have fazed the Victorian photographer
Who neglected to say *watch the birdie*
Whilst adjusting his exposure.

Gaslight bisects you face
As you take stock,
Looking over his shoulder - and mine.
At four already your own person.
(Ninety years still on the clock.)

Programmed to outpace
In life's marathon
Your grievously afflicted generation;
Called by God, or someone,
To his top division,

With your steadfast gaze
That can endorse
Life's duality: darkness and light.
You offer your own testimony.

From your still centre you have set course.

MY GODMOTHER

I like the scraps that fall from the leaves of old books
By unfashionable writers; books with sepia dedications
And scuffed spines: *Lavengro; Unto This Last.*
Books banished to dark shelves on silent upstairs landings
By families who have rooted themselves in one place:
A Serious Call to a Devout and Holy Life;
Taken down to be dusted, not read.
Snap their pages, making the motes fly -
The past drops out on a postcard from Ventnor.

I have found a four-leaved clover, still green,
Between two *Sonnets from the Portugese.*
There seemed more eloquence in that pressed token
Than in all the ardour of Mrs Browning;
And folded small, tucked in *The Romany Rye*
A page from a lined schoolbook; a child's hand:
'Dear Mr Editor, I hope you don't mind ...'
There courage failed, or resolution.
The pencil slides. The author drew a cat.

Sartor Resartus (the tailor patched), clothbound
In the Everyman edition of nineteen thirteen
Yields a sheet torn from a leger: 'Telephone Stringer.
Mother (if not too late) would like to have
The East Room Blinds (Venetian) changed to green.'
I note the flowing hand of my godmother
- Dutiful daughter, freshly fledged from the schoolroom,
Obedient to her mother's beck and call.

The family had taken Blackmoor Park
To live among a better sort of person
Where contacts could be made of the right sort
And wealth acquire the patina of age.
What hustle and bustle through the lofty rooms
To beeswax floors and roll out Turkey rugs,

Pour over catalogues from Maples Stores
And cram the mansion like a honeycomb,
A sweet snare, to entrap hearts!
In that heady year of expectation
Before the lamps went out all over Europe.

There were three grown sons - and the girl.

And there was Stringer. Did he, too, go to the wars
To fall at Passchendaele or Gallipoli?
Or did age spare him to shake out shrouds
Over mute cabinets and chiffoniers
To scatter camphor on the Turkey rugs
And draw the East Room blinds (Venetian - green?)
Against the shafts of unendurable brightness
In that grey mansion of desolation?

It is a mother's privilege to mourn,
Howl like the she-wolf, crazed with lamentation.
'She will know her duty,' they said of the girl.

My godmother had dreamed of cap and gown;
But making a virtue of necessity
She donned her old hand-me-down life
And lived with grace till she met God
Who honed her spirit sharp as a razor.

Staff at Blackmoor Park 1913

ANGELA *1928 - 1983*

September is when the year quickens
And each September
Marks a beginning.

So you came,
Hobbledy-hop
To the school door,

The balls of your feet
Taking the weight
From that bandaged knee.

- Such tenderness you had,
As if the act of walking
Might damage the earth.

And yet there was always
That diffidence about you,
That quiet watchfulness,

As of a guest, uncertain
Of a welcome at the feast;
Taking nothing for granted.

And thus you arrived
At where I was waiting
For something to happen.

What subtle chemistry
Kindles recognition?
Ignites friendship?

In our panamas and blazers
We saluted one another,
Feeling our future unroll.

Miscellany

SO I SAID ....

So I said - what I need is a time-share husband.
(Overheard at the Safeways checkout)

Oh my God, what had I said?
A time-share husband? What a nerve!
AGREE TO SHARE THE MAN I'D WED?
Apportion him I'd sworn to serve?

But what I mean to say is this:
If I could be his time-share wife
The freedom would be utter bliss!
How smoothly I'd get on with life!

You see, my job's in real estate
Which means I'm always on the trot.
Surveying flatlets is my fate
(No time to clean the one I've got.)

- Of course his work is far more grand,
Compared to him I'm dim and slow.
He shows such brilliant sleight of hand
- He is a City man you know.

Still, though my role is rather trad,
To be a wife still carries weight
And I know several who'd be glad
With me to share my wifely state.

Oh, what a burden off my mind
To shed this load of guilt and blame!
A substitute would be as kind
- Convenience foods taste much the same.

He's not exactly keen, you know,
Not into sex an awful lot.
He sometimes strokes me with his toe
- He needs his sleep no matter what.

But more than all, he needs to feel
That every piece is in its place
With someone home to cook a meal
And serve it with his mother's face.

How can I bear my life's dilution?
The way we live is quite insane!
He'd never spot the substitution
And I could be myself again.

SONG OF THE 'SIXTIES

Easing the company Cresta into the carport
  He switched himself off.
Decerebrated - Christ, how tired he was!
  He'd had about enough.

Time to blot out the Trotskyist shop steward,
  Civil, Moscow-trained
Weasel in a pale blue suit, swivel-eyed
  Dodgy, but sustained

By age-old grievances in talking crap.
  Yes - time to switch off.
It had been no worse than any other day
  But it had been - rough.

On the wall-to-wall fitted carpeting
  (Three-quarters paid)
Beside the splay-legged table his wife was waiting
  With the tea things laid.

And he - free-wheeling into the sitting room
  By custom, kissed.
Absently aiming pursed up lips for loving,
  Absently missed.

And no help came to her from the goggle faces
  On the twenty-inch screen.
Like his, their lives happened in other places
  She'd never seen.

Oh forgotten, far off university days
  When he, less wise,
Had almost drowned in grey amazing pools
  Of her grey eyes.

THE LARK

An absurd lark,
A ridiculous, thin bird,
Drank from a March puddle
In Greenan Road.

Brittle as a cornflake,
Bobbing, hopping about,
Zig-zagging in the wind,
Two fingers could crunch it.

Seeds and rainwater -
Is that all it takes
To power its ascending?
Fuel that immortal song?

WITTGENSTEIN

Famous for fifteen minutes?
That's never happened to me
Though I once met Wittgenstein.
- To be honest, he didn't impress me.

He wore a brown suit as I recall
Of wartime Utility cut;
His trousers bagged at the knee;
His collar was dusted with dandruff.

Swakeleys Road, Ickenham, Uxbridge,
Was the place where we met;
The home of my best friend.
- The house number escapes me.

He peered at me through thick lenses
As I offered him my hand.
His hair stood up in spikes.
- To be truthful, I'd never heard of him.

My friend's brother, a medic
With Byronic brown eyes
Like that poet, was in thrall to his sister
- An obstacle I'd failed to appreciate.

Wittgenstein, I dare say,
Had sized up the situation,
Which may have accounted
For his melancholy gaze.

The world of the happy is quite different
From that of the unhappy. So he'd written.
And whereof one cannot speak
Therefore one must be silent.

How green I was at seventeen!
Misreading the signals;
Soaking up the silence
With my starling chitter-chatter.

NOVEMBER CHRYSANTHEMUMS

In the lemon light between snow showers
She went out to hear the chrysanthemums
Roaring in their tawny throats;
Rallying the sun,
Challenging summer
To a last stand.

HOSPITAL NIGHTS

Sleepless in hospital after an operation I recited all the nursery rhymes I could remember. These macabre versions scribbled onto the backs of my 'Get Well' cards cheered me up a lot.

All night blackbirds screamed in her head,
Called the King, but he was fled,
Cut the crust, the birds were dead.
    Fly little dickie-bird, fly.

All night long and round and round
Where was Tom Tiddler found?
Boxed and buried underground.
    Fly little dickie-bird, fly.

Wee Willie Winkie tripped and fell,
Caught his foot in pussy's well,
Took a header, ding dong bell.
    Fly little dickie-bird, fly.

See-saw, Johnny's new boss
Fixed him to an iron cross,
Necklaced him with an albatross.
    Fly little dickie-bird, fly.

Poor Jack, poor Jill, went up the glen,
Ran into ten thousand men.
They never came down again.
    Fly little dickie-bird, fly.

Baa baa black sheep, musn't look,
Flayed and hanging from a hook
Eyes pecked clean by raven and rook.
    Fly little dickie-bird, fly.

Humpty Dumpty fell down thud,
Spilled his carrion on the road,
The King's men cantered through his blood.
    Fly little dickie-bird, fly.

Row, row, down the stream,
Don't heed the blackbirds' scream,
Their deaths you'll not redeem.
    Fly little dickie-bird, fly.

FEBRUARY 1991
Rhosgyll Fawr

The Gulf War injected new words and phrases
into our vocabulary.

i. CLEARING BRAMBLES FROM THE ISLAND

This island is a war zone:
Brambles taking off on their missions
Selecting targets of opportunity
From emplacements deep underground.

This half acre has been overrun
By forces with superior weaponry
Inflicting desired damage:
On touchdown an explosion of roots.

For his ground offensive
The enemy is well dug in;
His battle strategy
Encroachment by stealth.

I continue to hit him
With everything I've got.
It will be a long war.
Chemicals cannot be ruled out.

ii. FIELDFARES

A flock of fieldfares
Targetting the holly.
The tree trembles,
Its blurred silhouette
An explosion of wings.

iii. COOTS

Coots have a poor reputation,
Their couplings are violent,
They drown ducklings for sport.
Like humans they are quarrelsome,
They attack their own kind.

White-visored knights
Scudding between ice floes.
Yes - *scudding* is a good word for coots.

iv. SWANS

Out on the lake,
On melting ice floes,
A pair of brilliant swans
Puddle their own reflections:
Two swans making four.
- Forget war.

v. FEBRUARY SUN

Low in the West
The enormous sun
Followed me home.

At every step
My tawny giant
Kept pace with me.

Entering the wood,
Dark ash boles
Fractured his face.

Blackthorn thickets
Tore him to tatters
- Still he came on

My bold sun!
Crossing open pasture
I thought him mended

Till I saw
The windows of my house
Awash with his blood.

EARTHQUAKE

January 30 2001

i.

In a faraway land,
Fighting for breath under rubble,
A boy chips away at concrete
To free his crushed leg.

Airlifted in,
A young Russian doctor,
- A woman, small and steeled -
Is counselling amputation.
A leg for a life, but
A surgeon cannot be found.

One hour of daylight left,
One hour;
Light and time ebbing
- Twenty thousand dead,
But here one life, one child.

A beacon.

And one young woman
Willing it to burn on:
To have it continue.

ii.

They got him out, that one.
- She took off his leg, and
Hauled up the rest of him.

He's doing well, they say.

When his senses return
He will learn of a sister
Dug out alive,
Of a mother, father
(And his right leg)
All smashed to smithereens
In that rubblefield,
So lately a town.

And then he must learn
To get on with his life.

The Third Age

MUMMY CALLING

Well, darling, I've arrived - whole, but exhausted
- There was a pile-up near York. Yes. Two young people
Killed, I believe. Speeding. A youth and some girl.
Driving is seldom a pleasure nowadays
But here I am. And now I must tell you.

It's much worse than we thought, really much worse
And something will have to be done. She is virtually
Alone in this great barracks of a house
Which cannot be allowed. Someone must tell her
How selfish it is of her to live like this,
How pig-headed. Oh - the selfishness of the old!

It seems she had some kind of an attack.
In the night, feeling sick, she left her bed
And fumbling her way across the landing
Reached the stairhead and managed to call out.
That woman we engaged? Oh - she is deaf,
She slept on. She is only a pitman's wife
And quite unsuitable. How one can be deceived!

Mother it seems collapsed upon the landing
And lay some hours before the woman found her.
It was her heart. No one has dared tell her
But she must be told. Her doctor is a fool,
He has no right to keep her in ignorance
And expect us to bear the responsibility.

The way she has been living I won't dwell on.
The pong! She has no one to keep her decent
And at night must painfully push off her stockings
With her stick. For decency's sake she must be told
- Her obstinacy reflects upon us all.

What's that you say? Your uncle at Caputh?
One naturally assumed that Julian
Living so near, would take his mother in.
That obscene baby! Those were his own words.
Almost every week I call on her
- Last March I pruned her roses. His obligation
Ends in the rose garden, although his house
Is crammed with everything of hers unravaged
By beetle and worm. Yes - woodworm and beetle
Inherit this house.

Her collie puppy, Dell,
Follows me everywhere. She fouls the old schoolroom
But Mother is indifferent. *No one visits*
Here any more, she says. *And Dell's my girlie.*
I can't stay more than two days, I'm returning
The day after tomorrow. In the meantime
Her doctor must be seen - also her lawyer.
What's that you say?
No - it's not possible.
Besides, she would not come. It's more than time
Unknotted our blood tie. I have been spilled,
Spilled. We are hollow women and this house,
This empty shell where I poured out my days
Once, under the shadow of her eye:
This empty, empty place - unhaunted even,
Because childhood and girlhood were drained
Here. What's that you say?
I said this house
Reeks of spent years and now there's nothing more
That can be done. Only, she must be told.

This - Home - is not at all an institution
And we shall all feel happier for her sake
Knowing she's in good hands. I think I'll tell her
Later this evening, when I've warmed her milk.

THE OLD LADY'S SONG

I'm still waiting for my life to begin,
 Sang the old lady as she lay dying.
- Oh why has my time been so thin?
  And why am I crying?

I was too obliging, too compliant,
  She sang low from her high hospital cot.
- Timid, when I should have been defiant,
  Now I've had my lot.

Oh why did I burn so for my father?
  The old lady sang. - Why cling to my mother?
Bruising a heart I'd have rather
  Kept whole for some other.

All the apples in my basket turned rotten
  Sang the old lady plaintively.
- Some got silk, satin, or cotton,
  With just rags left for me.

I'm still waiting for the pantomime to begin,
  She sang soft under the bare strip lights.
Now it's gone so quiet you could drop a pin.
  - I was never one for fights,

They all said I wouldn't hurt a fly,
  She whispered as they wheeled in the tea trolley.
 - If that's a fact I'd like the chance to try
   Just one bit of folly.

Tuesdays and Fridays God comes in his white coat,
  She sang loud, feeling the sheet go wet.
Bugger's never even asked to see my throat!
  He can't want me just yet.

MANSEL'S VISION

Welcome, dear friend, I hoped you might drop in.
A match now, to the fire? You'll take some tea?
No trouble - see - legs perfectly steady.
A clean bill of health from the hospital
Though a close call; teetering on the brink
Of cancellation; almost cast off to face
Oblivion after fourscore turbulent years.

Yet here I am! A robust constitution,
Aided by scientific wizardry
Has called me back from the everlasting sleep
To share what was for me a marvellous time
- I mean in the literal sense: a time of marvels.

Sit there my dear. China or Indian?
The old keep pots of gold nobody wants
But tea - now there's a comfort and a blessing!
So bear with me, while I sketch out my vision.

My bypass operation, undertaken
In an emergency, when I already
Was weak, resulted in a period
In which I was sedated and at best
In semi-conscious mode. Nevertheless
I still retained an intelligible sense
Of being alive, only because my mind
Experienced and recorded sequences
Of unforgettable acuity.

Deprived of oxygen, my brain explored
Kaleidoscopic vistas unsurpassed
In brilliant variety and colour,
Their boundaries moving, so the pattern flowed,
Forming elaborate mosaics, transcending
All art forms I had known.

And I recall
Further miraculous forms approximating
To mobile landscapes or deep ocean currents
Patterned in temporary symmetries
Over a moving background, blue and green.

Do I bore you? Permit me to digress.
(My thoughts wheel and cut like harcs in a cornfield.)

The late Sir Freddy Ayer, sometime Professor
Of Logic at Oxford University,
Shortly before his end experienced
While under medical examination
A four-minute death. Deeply unconscious
He yet retained a vivid memory
Of his impressions, afterwards rendering
(Upon successful resuscitation)
A notable account, remarkable
For one habitually sceptical,
Conjecturing how his experiences
Might have continued beyond his death.

What did he mean, this lifelong rationalist?
Did he posit a soul? Mind without matter
Still sentient following physical decay?
An essence long denied? When the bell tolled
For him, had his feet faltered?

I must laugh circumspectly, fearing to choke,
For there's far more outside our galaxy
Than we can dream of when we fashion gods
Too like ourselves, too close for any comfort,
Whose tribal laws give substance to our fears,
Whose tribal masks cover a timorous face.

You are silent. Seek not to comfort the old.
Living our pared-down lives, stripped of excess
We are bold, only needing to wag our tongues;
Abandoning the answers we retain
The universal questions; the old riddles.

THE OLD ARE NOT LIKE US

This poem is part of an earlier draft of 'Mansel's Vision'

The old are not like us, their bones sing,
Their thoughts wheel and cut like hares in a cornfield.

Abandoning the answers, they retain
The universal questions, the old riddles.

Seek not to comfort the old, they are bold,
But must laugh circumspectly, fearing to choke.

Living their pared-down lives, stripped of excess
- Only needing to wag their tongues.

The old have pots of gold nobody wants
Yet may confound us with their fine unpicking -
Substantiality to threads of spray.

WHEN I AM OLD I SHALL GROW ROSES

When I am old I shall grow roses,
I shall take a town house in Ludlow or Abergavenny
Which has a garden with mellow walls
And crumbled brick paths to soak up the sun
And I shall go for bust at Midsummer.

I shall have no truck with the pity of spring,
The leveret's scream, the young cuckoo in the nest,
I shall not weep for the fading of the daffodils,
I shall ditch my rubber galoshes.

I shall not plan for an orderly succession,
I shall be improvident like the late swallows,
My plantings will be all higgledy-piggledy,
I shall lump everything together.

Some days I shall take a rose between my teeth like a matador
And make rude noises to frighten the ladybirds.
Horse manure will be barrowed through my house.
And when inclined I shall play the murderess,
I shall boil rhubarb leaves to make a strong poison,
My fine nozzle will spray on death.

I shall keep a crystal bowl for the clotted petals of my favourites -
Queen of Denmark, Mermaid, Roserie de l'Hay -
My pergolas toppling with their weight of scent
I shall live in a torrent of summer.

I shall be both priestess and princess.
I shall make an arbour with a high stone seat.
As day fades I shall call up my roses,
The air of my garden will be thick with their names.

My tongue will wrap itself round the lovely words -
Danse de Feu, Etoile de Hollande, Compassion,
Ispahan, Fantin Latour, Mutabilis,
The unbearable echoes of the *Bourbons*.

I shall dwell in my Paradise garden
And take no heed for the morrow,
My passionate flame still aflicker
Behind the terrible, dry, lizard's smile

A few Words with Myself

A WORD WITH MYSELF

Can't you do better?
-Can't you do it any better?

Half-feeling,
Half-giving,
Half-alive,
Only half-living,

Feeding little flames with matchsticks,
Feeding flames with little matchsticks,
Your half-heart safety-pinned?

Can't you crash out?
Unwind?
Learn to fly?
Launch yourself
Into the wind?

One day you'll be found out.
One day they'll expose you
(Your gifts measured in teaspoons).

Purgatory yawns
For people like you.
Your insouciance
Won't work there.

HATE IS -

Thou shalt love thy neighbour as thyself

Hate is hard as a
rotten nut.
Weighs heavy.
A lead meal.

Hate corrodes,
feels like rust
scorching the throat.

Hate is a sickness, a
smouldering flame, damp fire,
acid smarting smoke.

Hate is a windowless room
you've locked yourself into.

Hate is stealthy, a cancer eating holes
Out of itself.

Hate is a soured wine.
A murderous sunset.
A poisoned, deadly pollen.

Hate crawls, slithers,
A lava-flow of ashes.

Hate is a pit you've dug for yourself.
A self-inflicted wound.

Hate is diminution.
Man without God.
Me without you.

THE NIGHT WATCHMEN

Put out the light and let the demons come in
With their crumpled faces, their raw tongues, their breath like tar,
Bid them welcome, you shall not stay their din,
They will find you wherever you are.

Beneath your bed they slide, arching their huge
Raddled backs to make your mattress pitch
- So you ride them, you must ride, for no subterfuge
Will shift them, or get you off, you can't hitch

Or rein them - and there are others, quite small,
That will slip under your eyelids to lodge like lice
Waxing fat on tears, so at each nightfall
- Meal-soft bodies clogging every orifice -

Your heart's runnels are choked up and each
Heartbeat trammelled and every harsh breath
Trawled through deeps of desolation, to teach
You the pity of living, comfort of death.

Then last, at their slow pace, with no show
Of haste, but coming on like the rough
Weather from the west, you will know
Them, the night watchmen, sent to call your bluff.

Put out the light, for they are come with their
Dark lanterns to stand vigil round your bed
And through the dog-watch keep you in their care,
Two at your feet, two at your head.

BIRD CHERRY

I would like to be the bird cherry,
Yes - I would like to be that tree

At the lakeside, brightening
The cold loom of a northern Spring,
Shaken with gentle laughter
At my own blossoming,
At my joy in the Spring.

Yes - I would like to feel
The sweet sap come up,
To drink deep, deep,
From Earth's great loving cup
And feel the Spring rush up.

To shake milky tassels
Signalling surprise! surprise!
Astonishing the wayfarer,
Innocently drawing his eyes,
Taking him by surprise.

Poised, as if freshly alighted,
Trembling with merriment
At the lakeside, quivering
At my own heart's content
A-quiver with merriment.

My flowering racemes innocent
Of their bitter berry,
Of bird-thirst in Winter
Slaked by my cherry
By my black bitter berry.

ALL CLEAR

As if you could lean out and finger them,
As if clear air had rinsed away distance
So you could set upon your window-sill
The ewes and the lambs.
As if a finger nail
Could scratch away the furse from distant hills
Or the palm of a hand rest in their hollows.

As if the linen, cracking on the line
In a March wind,
Battered and bruised the headland
Full three miles distant.
As if you felt as if your self were stretched upon a line
And like the retted flax set out to bleach
And like rinsed linen to crack and to shine.